MOVING & GROOVING
to FILLMORE'S BEAT

written by Rachel Werner
illustrated by Jerrard K. Polk

CAPSTONE EDITIONS
a capstone imprint

To Phoebe, the absolute best part
of my existence thus far. —R.W.

To Jerry and Vanessa, I am forever grateful
for your tutelage and example.—J.K.P.

Published by Capstone Editions, an imprint of Capstone
1710 Roe Crest Drive, North Mankato, Minnesota 56003
capstonepub.com

Library of Congress Cataloging-in-Publication Data
is available on the Library of Congress website
ISBN: 9781684467631 (hardcover)
ISBN: 9781684467587 (paperback)
ISBN: 9781684467594 (ebook PDF)

Summary: Creativity fills the air in the Fillmore District,
bringing everyone together—with no exceptions.

Printed and bound in China. PO5377

Along old **Geary Boulevard,**
at number 1-8-0-5,
stood a **grand ballroom.**

It was the place to **jive.**

Tempos **boomed** and **grooved**,
carrying dreams as full as the **moon**.
And everyone knew that this venue

was filled with **MAGIC.**

'Cause the Fillmore crew
played the **best tunes.**

Their **music** became the **glue**,
and set the **mood**.

1960s

Drawing pals on **foot,**

by **cable car,**

or **trolley.**

To a location, they could

dance . . . sing . . .

and sow harmony.

With hands and feet
moving and **grooving,**
music poured from open windows
and through closed doors.

Flowing into the streets . . .

Freckled, golden, honey skin.

Caramel, cinnamon, and cocoa.

1970s

All faces were **welcomed**
and **appreciated.**

Each Fillmore friend
brought a gift to share . . .

Maya's words rose.

Isaacs's bow stirred.

Etta's vocals lifted.

John's notes jazzed.

Carlos's strums moved.

Sugar Pie's feet flipped.

Together, filling the neighborhood with awe and joy.

Piece by piece, hand in hand,
adding voices **BIG and small.**

Instruments sent up a call,
that told them to be **proud**
of who they were **born to be.**

1980s

Together, they created

an oasis for art...

for activism . . .

for acceptance.

They created **books,**

music,

paintings,

poems,

and took **photos.**

Art moving hearts toward **PEACE.**

With stories, pictures, and songs,
they **broke down** walls
and turned them into **bridges.**

1990s

Time passed, as time will do . . .

Some friends stayed rooted in San Francisco.

Others sought new adventures far away.

But the Fillmore kept on jiving.

New creators came, their **voices rising.**
These blocks stayed **alive** as concerts,
then festivals, brought crowds to the streets.

Present Day

Rhymes and **rhythms** blazed
like **beacons**
in Harlem of the West.

Thanks to a legendary chorus
history should **not forget.**

The Fillmore District's Creative Legacy

The Fillmore District first became popular after the 1906 earthquake in San Francisco, California. It was one of the few neighborhoods in the city that remained standing after the disaster. What had once been mostly residential housing for Jewish immigrants soon began to attract new businesses and populations, including Black, Japanese, and Mexican families.

As word spread about the inclusive nature of the neighborhood, aspiring and famous artists and entertainers gravitated there. The Black community in particular grew and thrived.

With the glamorous concert hall as its centerpiece, the Fillmore District became known for its bustling music scene. Famous musicians from around the country appeared onstage. Its vibrant music scene endures today, both on the Fillmore Auditorium stage and during the annual Fillmore Street Jazz Festival.

The artists at the Fillmore promoted a message of inclusion, rejecting judgment based on race, ethnicity, gender, and religion. They showed that anyone can cultivate hubs of community. We can learn from residents of diverse neighborhoods about what it means to live intentionally alongside those with identities, traditions, and languages different from our own.

Famous Artists at the Fillmore

Maya Angelou: Best known for poems describing the triumphs and challenges of being Black in America, Maya Angelou spent her life expressing creativity through writing, singing, dancing, and acting.

Mel Blanc: An actor and radio star, Mel Blanc was most famous for being the voices of Bugs Bunny, Daffy Duck, Porky Pig, and several other Looney Tunes characters.

Sugar Pie DeSanto: A biracial rhythm and blues singer and songwriter, Sugar Pie DeSanto's lively dance routines with handstands made her a trendsetter in the 1960s.

John Handy: A talented jazz musician, John Handy mastered at least six different instruments throughout his lengthy career.

Etta James: Considered by many to be the "Matriarch of the Blues," Etta James was one of the first women to be inducted into the Rock and Roll Hall of Fame.

David Johnson: The first Black student of legendary photographer Ansel Adams, David Johnson would become the most famous photographer to ever take pictures of the Fillmore District.

Carlos Santana: Having sold nearly 80 million albums during his career, this Mexican American guitarist, drummer, and singer is the founder of the band Santana and the nonprofit organization the Milagro "Miracle" Foundation.

Nyogen Senzaki: A Japanese monk, Nyogen Senzaki provided the first documented instruction of Zen Buddhism in the United States.

Isaac Stern: A Jewish virtuoso violinist, Isaac Stern became one of the most celebrated classical musicians of the twentieth century.

About the Author

Rachel Werner is on faculty for Lighthouse Writers Workshop in Denver, Hugo House in Seattle, and The Loft Literary Center in Minneapolis. A regular book reviewer for Shelf Awareness, she has contributed print, photography, and video content to many projects. Rachel is the founder of The Little Book Project WI, a community arts nonprofit committed to pursuing social justice through narrative. She lives in Madison, Wisconsin, where she serves on the board of Monroe Street Arts Center.

About the Illustrator

Jerrard K. Polk has been drawing all his life. He received his professional start as an artist at the age of 15 and was educated at The Art Institute of Charlotte in North Carolina. His love of books and poetry was encouraged by his mother, a librarian. Today, he enjoys sharing his fondness for art and entrepreneurship with children. He is greatly inspired by jazz and the dapper fashions of its innovators. He has illustrated several books for children, including *The Story of John Lewis*, *Black Inventors*, and *A Child's Introduction to Jazz*.